Gardening

Wildlife Gardens

Lori Kinstad Pupeza

ABDO Publishing Company

visit us at
www.abdopub.com

Published by ABDO Publishing Company 4940 Viking Drive, Edina, Minnesota 55435.
Copyright © 2002 by Abdo Consulting Group, Inc. International copyrights reserved in
all countries. No part of this book may be reproduced in any form without written
permission from the publisher.
Printed in the United States.

Photo credits: Corbis, Corel
Contributing editors: Bob Italia, Tamara L. Britton, Kate A. Furlong, Kristin Van Cleaf
Book design and graphics: Neil Klinepier

Library of Congress Cataloging-in-Publication Data

Pupeza, Lori Kinstad.
    Wildlife gardens / Lori Kinstad Pupeza.
       p.   cm. -- (Gardening)
    Includes index.
    Summary: Provides information on choosing a site for a garden, picking plants that
will attract birds, butterflies, and other animals, and caring for your garden.
    ISBN 1-57765-032-8
    1. Gardening to attract wildlife--Juvenile literature. [1. Gardening.
  2. Wildlife attracting.] I. Title. II. Series: Pupeza, Lori Kinstead.
  Gardening.
  QL59.P87   2000
  639.9'2--dc21   98-16910
                                         CIP
                                         AC

Dial Before You Dig

Before digging in your yard with a motorized tiller, call your local utility
company to determine the location of underground utility lines.

Contents

Wildlife Gardens

Plants and animals live together in nature. Some plants naturally attract wildlife. Just a small area of land filled with the right plants will bring lots of birds, bees, and butterflies to your yard.

You'll need a few gardening tools and supplies to get started. Then you will need to select your garden's location, prepare the soil, and pick out your plants.

Your garden will need care and maintenance. Watering and pulling weeds are big jobs. You will also need to provide food and homes for your animals and insects. But, growing a wildlife garden is worth the work. It will allow you to see nature in your own backyard!

Gardening Tools

Turning Soil & Weeding

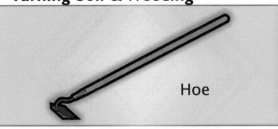

Hoe

Raking

Garden Rake

Watering

Watering Can

Hose

Planting

Trowel

Digging

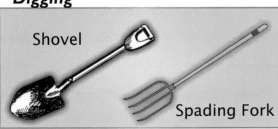

Shovel

Spading Fork

Pest Control

Sprayer

A Place for a Garden

When picking a location for your wildlife garden, look for a sunny area. Most plants need a lot of sunlight. But, some plants grow well in shade. So if your yard only has shady spots, they will work, too.

If your yard is hilly, put your garden at the top of a hill, rather than at the bottom. Water doesn't drain well from the bottom of a hill. Plants have a greater chance of rotting or getting diseases if they sit in water.

When choosing a location for your garden, pick an area that is easy to get to. This makes it easier to do maintenance such as watering and weeding.

Make sure to plant your garden near a source of water!

Making Plans

There are many decisions to make about your garden before you dig into the dirt. How big will your garden be? What kinds of plants would you like to grow? What kinds of wildlife would you like to attract to your garden?

To decide what size garden to plan, think about how many plants you want to grow, and how much work you want to do. A three by five foot (1 by 1.5 m) garden is a good size to start with. This is enough space for several different kinds of plants, and you will not have to do much weeding.

After you decide on the size of your garden, think about where to place the plants. To make planning more fun, draw your plans on a piece of paper. Remember to make room for a birdbath, bird and butterfly houses, and feeders, too.

Birds like to take baths! A birdbath in your wildlife garden will bring many kinds of birds to your yard.

Choosing Plants

To create a successful wildlife garden, pick out your plants and flowers carefully. Birds and insects are attracted to sweet-smelling flower blooms, fruits, and berries.

When you're at the **nursery** or garden center, look on the back of seed packets or on the markers in the **seedlings'** pots. They will tell you whether the plants attract butterflies or other wildlife.

You should decide if you want perennials, biennials, or annuals. Perennials grow back each spring. Biennials live for two summers and die during the second winter. Annuals bloom for one summer and then die.

You will also need to determine the date of the last frost in your climate. Check the frost zone map to make sure the danger of frost has passed in your area.

Frost Zones

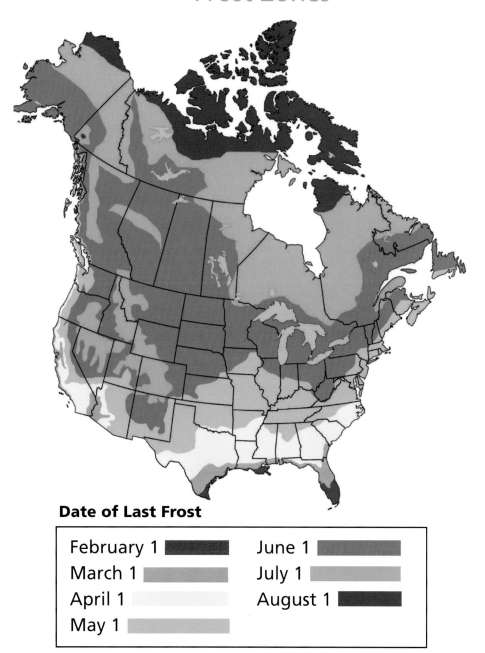

Date of Last Frost

February 1	June 1
March 1	July 1
April 1	August 1
May 1	

Preparing Soil

Once you have a garden planned, it's time to get the soil ready. The first step is to remove any grass, weeds, and rocks from the area.

Next, check to see what kind of soil you have in your yard. If you have dry, sandy soil, mix **peat moss** into it. This will help the soil hold water. If your soil seems thick or clay-like, add **manure** to it. This will help your garden drain excess water better.

Plants grow best in topsoil that has been **tilled**. A motorized tiller works best. But you can also till with a shovel or hoe. Tilling the top 8 to 12 inches (20 to 30 cm) of topsoil allows your plants to easily grow roots and soak up water.

Opposite page: Ask an adult to help if you are tilling your garden with a motorized tiller.

Seeds & Seedlings

There are many ways to plant a garden. You can buy seeds and plant them directly into the soil. Or, you can buy **seedlings**. Seedlings are usually two to six inches (5 to 15 cm) tall, and have already grown roots. Both seeds and seedlings are easy to plant.

To plant seeds, first read the seed package to determine how deep and how close together to plant them. Then, dig a trench, drop in the seeds, and cover them with soil. Water the seeds right away. Watering them regularly helps them to **germinate.**

COSMOS

These early-blooming, daisy-like flowers will bloom until frost.

Plant Height	Plant Spacing	Planting Depth	Days to Germination
3-4 ft.	12-15 in.	1/4 in.	5-10

PLANTING INSTRUCTIONS
Plant in sunny location. Cosmos will grow in poor soil.

When to Plant Outdoors

	May-June
	April-June
	March-June
	Jan.-June
	Jan.-Dec.

Seed packages contain useful information such as when to plant the seeds, how much to water them, and how long they will need to become mature plants.

If you buy **seedlings**, water them as soon as you get home. Then, dig a hole in the ground where the seedling will go. Put the plant into the hole, and spread dirt around the roots. Be sure the base of the plant sits even with the ground. Then water the seedling again.

Planting seedlings

Watering

Every plant needs water to live. The amount of water to give a plant depends on how much it needs and how much rain your area gets. You will learn to tell when your plants need water by tending your garden every day.

If your garden's soil is light colored and dusty, it needs water. Soil that is dark colored doesn't need to be watered. Sticking your finger an inch (2.5 cm) into the soil is also a good way to tell whether the soil is moist or dry.

Overwatering can harm your garden. The stem of a plant shouldn't sit in water. This might cause mold or **fungus** to grow on the plant's stem and kill it. Watering the right amount regularly will give you strong plants and long-lasting blooms.

Your garden will need
water to grow.

Feeding

Water isn't the only thing plants need to grow. They also need **minerals** and **nutrients** from the soil. A good way to add nutrients to your garden's soil is to use **fertilizer**.

Compost is a natural fertilizer. It is made of decomposed **organic** materials. Some gardeners make their own compost. You can also buy it at a garden center. To use compost, mix it into your garden's soil.

Garden centers also sell chemical fertilizers. Most fertilizer can be sprinkled around the base of the plant or mixed in with the garden soil. But, too much fertilizer can harm your plants. Read the instructions on the fertilizer container and ask an adult to help you with fertilizing.

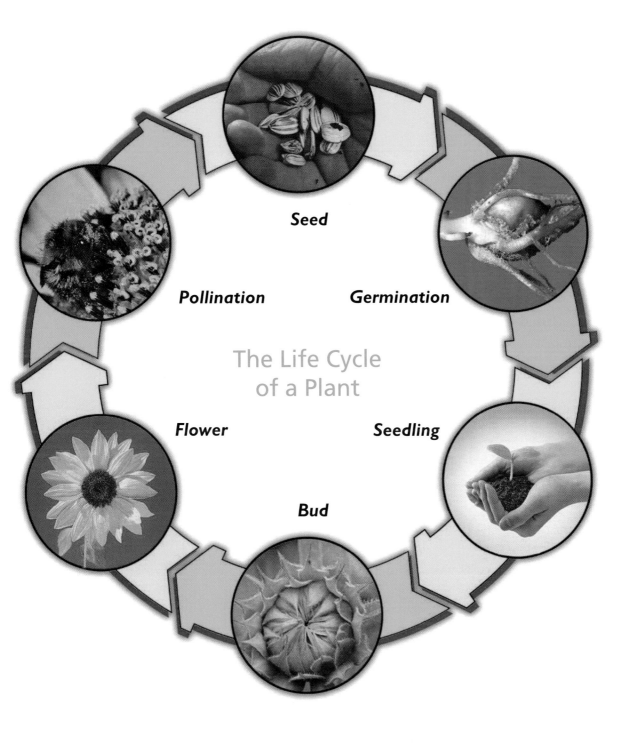

Seed

Pollination

Germination

The Life Cycle
of a Plant

Flower

Seedling

Bud

Weeding

Once your garden begins to grow, you'll need to maintain it. Weeding is an important job. Weeds steal water and **nutrients** from your plants.

To prevent weeds from competing with your plants, pull each weed out from its base. Make sure to get the roots. If you leave the roots, the weed will grow back.

Another way to remove weeds is with chemicals. Garden centers sell chemicals you can spray on weeds. But chemicals aren't healthy for the environment, or for the animals you want to attract to your garden.

A safer way to keep weeds out of your garden is to use mulch. To mulch your garden, place grass clippings, straw, or wood chips on the dirt around your flowers. This will stop weeds from growing, and keep the sun from drying out the soil.

When pulling weeds, be sure to get the roots so they will not grow back.

Garden Pests

Some of the wildlife attracted to your garden can be harmful. Animals such as deer or rabbits will want to eat your plants. To keep these animals out, build a three foot (1 m) fence around your garden.

A fence won't keep out all pests. Insects such as cutworms, aphids, Japanese beetles, and cabbage worms may still enter your garden. They eat garden plants, too.

How can you eliminate these garden pests? It's best to pick worms or insects from the plants by hand. You should pull out any badly damaged or diseased plants and throw them away.

Opposite page: Aphids are common garden pests. They can be removed from plants by spraying them with water.

Building a Bird House

Many birds will visit your wildlife garden. They will stay in your garden and eat harmful insects if you give them water and a place to sleep. An easy way to invite birds to your garden is to provide a bird house.

A simple way to make a bird house is to use a paper milk carton. First, rinse out the carton and tape the top closed. Then cut a one-inch (2.5 cm) hole in one of the sides. Directly below the hole, punch a small stick through the carton. This will be the perch.

Next, punch a hole through the top of the carton and run a string or wire through it. This will be used to hang the carton from a tree branch. Decorate the carton any way you like.

A milk carton bird house will attract more birds to your garden.

In the Fall

After the first freeze, your plants will turn brown and die. Pull the dead annual plants out of your garden. Trim away the dead stems and leaves on the perennials.

Next, spread leaves and grass clippings on the soil. This mulch layer will act like a blanket. It will protect your perennials over the cold winter months.

Many animals will come to depend on your wildlife garden for food and shelter. In some areas, many birds migrate south for the winter. But, other birds and animals stay.

You will need to continue to provide food and homes for the animals that stay. Supporting them during the winter ensures their survival, and that they will return to your garden in the spring.

In the fall, cut away dead plants and layer leaves on your garden.

A Few Good Flowers

There are many flowers and plants that will attract wildlife. The plants that grow best in your garden will change depending on your climate. Here is a list to get you started. All of these plants need full sun, and rich, well-drained soil.

Some plants are good at attracting bugs that **pollinate** flowers. Cosmos can grow up to six feet (2 m) tall, and attracts bees and butterflies. Achillea, sedum, black-eyed Susan, and coneflower are shorter, bushier flowers that also attract pollinators.

Hummingbirds are attracted to the brightly colored salvia flower. These tiny birds like its sweet **nectar**. Tall, yellow sunflowers also bring birds to a garden. Strawberry plants and most kinds of herbs attract birds, too.

Marigolds come in all different sizes and shapes, but they have a strong scent. Some animals don't like the smell of marigolds, so these flowers work best as a border around a vegetable garden.

Hummingbirds' wings beat so fast, they must eat every 15 to 20 minutes to maintain their energy level.

Glossary

fertilizer - a substance used to help plants grow.

fungus - a group of plants that lack flowers, leaves, and chlorophyll. Mold, mildew, and mushrooms are fungi.

germinate - to sprout and begin to grow.

manure - waste products from animals used as fertilizer.

mineral - a substance that is not animal or vegetable, occurs in nature, and has a defined chemical composition.

nectar - a sweet liquid formed by many flowers.

nursery - a place where plants, trees, and shrubs are grown for sale.

nutrients - something naturally found in soil that helps plants grow.

organic - material that is obtained from living things.

peat moss - a pale green moss that grows in swamps and bogs.

pollinate - to transfer pollen from one flower or plant to another.

seedling - a young plant grown from seed and not yet transplanted.

till - to prepare land for growing crops by turning over the soil to mix in air and nutrients.

Web Sites

National Wildlife Federation
http://www.nwf.org/habitats/
This site from the National Wildlife Federation is designed to help people create wildlife habitats. Includes step-by-step instructions for starting your backyard wildlife habitat.

Wildlife Gardens
http://www.wildlife-gardens.net
A newsletter for those who wish to preserve wildlife by providing habitats in their yards.

These sites are subject to change. Go to your favorite search engine and type in Wildlife Gardens for more sites.

Index